HOW MACHINES WORK

CONSTRUCTION VEHICLES

TERRY JENNINGS

A⁺

Smart Apple Media

Smart Apple Media is published by Black Rabbit Books
P.O. Box 3263, Mankato, Minnesota 56002

U.S. publication copyright © 2009 Black Rabbit Books. International copyright reserved
in all countries. No part of this book may be reproduced in any form without written
permission from the publisher.

Printed in Hong Kong

Library of Congress Cataloging-in-Publication Data

Jennings, Terry J.
    Construction vehicles / Terry Jennings.
    p. cm.—(Smart Apple Media—how machines work)
    Includes index.
    Summary: "Describes in detail construction vehicles used in digging, paving, and general construction, and how they
work"—Provided by publisher.
    ISBN 978-1-59920-293-8
    1. Earthmoving machinery—Juvenile literature. 2. Construction equipment—Juvenile literature. I. Title.
TA725.J46 2009
624.1'52—dc22

2008002400

Created by Q2AMedia
Series Editor: Honor Head
Book Editor: Harriet McGregor
Senior Art Director: Ashita Murgai
Designers: Harleen Mehta, Shilpi Sarkar
Picture Researchers: Amit Tigga, Poloumi Ghosh

All words in **bold** can be found in the Glossary on pages 30–31.

Web site information is correct at time of going to press. However, the publishers cannot
accept liability for any information or links found on third-party Web sites.

Picture credits
t=top b=bottom c=center l=left r=right m=middle
Cover Images: Volvo

Ljupco Smokovski/ Shutterstock: 4, Robert Harding Picture Library Ltd/ Alamy: 5tl, Jack Dagley Photography/
Shutterstock: 5tr, Semjonow Juri/ Shutterstock: 5b, Anton Gvozdikov/ Shutterstock: 6, Wally Stemberger/ Shutterstock: 7b, John
Deere: 8, Volvo: 9t, 9b, Albert H. Teich/ Shutterstock: 11t, Reino Hanninen/ Alamy: 11b, Gabe Palmer/ Alamy:12,
Bruce Burkhardt/ Flirt Collection/ Photolibrary: 13t, Anssi Ruuska/ Istockphoto: 14, Bjorn Heller/ Shutterstock: 15,
Lixxim/ Shutterstock: 17, Steven Robertson/ Istockphoto: 18, JoLin/ Shutterstock: 19, Comet, Zürich/ Nagra.ch 21b,
Robert Pernell/ Shutterstock: 22, Volvo: 23t, John Deere: 24, Volvo: 25t, 25b, Vögele America, Inc.: 26-27,
Maxim Loskuutov: 28, Dumitrescu Ciprian-Florin/ Shutterstock: 29t, Mikasa Construction Equipment: 29b

Q2AMedia Art Bank: 7t, 10, 13b, 15t, 16, 19, 20

9 8 7 6 5 4 3 2 1

CONTENTS

MIGHTY MACHINES

The huge machines that are used to build roads, bridges, tunnels, and buildings are construction vehicles. Many of them use levers and pulleys.

A **lever** is a tool that allows work to be done more easily. It does this by magnifying the effort that is put into lifting, pulling, pushing, or turning. The bigger the lever, the more the effort is increased. Bottle openers, wheelbarrows, and crowbars are all examples of simple levers.

▶ Levers help this powerful digger scoop up heavy soil and rubble, and lift it high in the air.

HOW LEVERS WORK

All levers involve effort, a fulcrum, and a load. The effort is the work done, such as lifting, pulling, and turning. The fulcrum is the place where the lever pivots or turns. The load is the object you want to move.

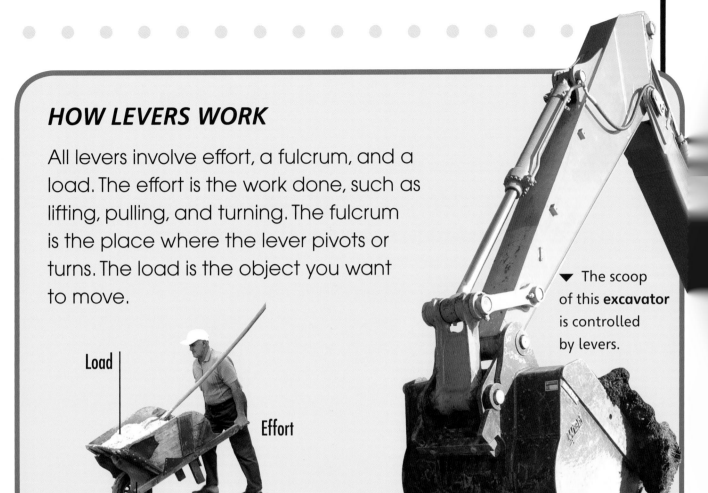

Load

Effort

Fulcrum

▼ The scoop of this **excavator** is controlled by levers.

PULLEYS

Another tool used by construction machines is the **pulley** (see page 14). The more pulleys used to lift a weight, the less effort it takes.

▼ Using pulleys, this mobile crane can lift weights of up to 220 tons (200 t).

Pulley blocks

Hook for lifting

DIGGERS AND LOADERS

Mechanical diggers need massive strength for scooping, lifting, and carrying. Huge hydraulic arms give them the power they need to break up soil and rubble.

In an excavator, **hydraulic** fluid moves a **piston** up and down a **cylinder**. When fluid is pumped into the top of the cylinder, the piston moves down and the dipper arm moves up. When liquid is pumped into the bottom of the cylinder, the piston moves up and the dipper arm moves down.

Piston

Cylinder

Dipper arm

DID YOU KNOW?
In one day, the world's largest excavator can dig a hole the size of a soccer field and more than 82 ft. (25 m) deep.

HOW A HYDRAULIC RAM WORKS

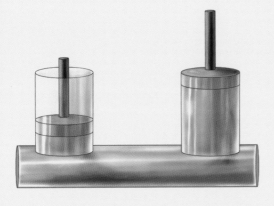

In a hydraulic system, force applied in one place is transferred to another place by squeezing a liquid. As hydraulic fluid is pumped into a cylinder, the small force at one end passes along the pipe and turns into a big force at the other end.

Hydraulic ram
Slides up and down to move the dipper arm and **bucket**

Dipper arm

Joint
Acts as a fulcrum

Bucket

▶ Machines such as this digger use a thin hydraulic fluid that does not freeze in cold weather.

SCOOP, LIFT, AND CARRY

A backhoe loader is a tractor, loader, and backhoe all in one. The loader at the front can scoop, lift, and carry. The backhoe at the rear of the machine can dig trenches and lift heavy loads. When the backhoe loader is working, hydraulic fluid pushes out **jacks** called **stabilizers**. These steady the machine and take the weight off the wheels and tires.

JOHN DEERE 710G BACKHOE LOADER

Specification

Engine:	6 cylinder diesel
Weight:	13 tons (12 t)
Lift capacity:	4.4 tons (4 t)
Digging depth:	17.7 ft (5.4 m)

Backhoe
Can stretch up, swivel around, and dig down

Tractor

Loader
Front loader bucket is shaped so it does not spill soil

Stabilizer
Steadies the machine and takes the weight off the wheels and tires

The backhoe loader has a powerful engine, large tires, and a cab with glass all the way around. The driver can turn the seat around to face the front or the back

RAMS AND JACKS

In construction machines, hydraulic systems move **rams** and jacks. A ram is a cylinder and piston that acts like the muscles of your arm. It pushes and moves parts around. Rams can be found on excavators. Jacks are also cylinders and pistons. They work like legs and feet to support and steady machines while they work.

▶ The driver needs controls to make the hydraulic systems work. These are the controls for the backhoe.

Control for backhoe and bucket

Control for the jacks

This backhoe loader is being used to dig a trench along a road before large concrete drainpipes are installed.

PILEDRIVING POWER!

Imagine the force needed to hammer huge steel and concrete rods into solid ground. Powerful machines called piledrivers do this work.

A piledriver works like a giant hammer. A heavy weight is lifted high into the air. The weight is dropped again and again onto steel or concrete **piles** to drive them into the ground.

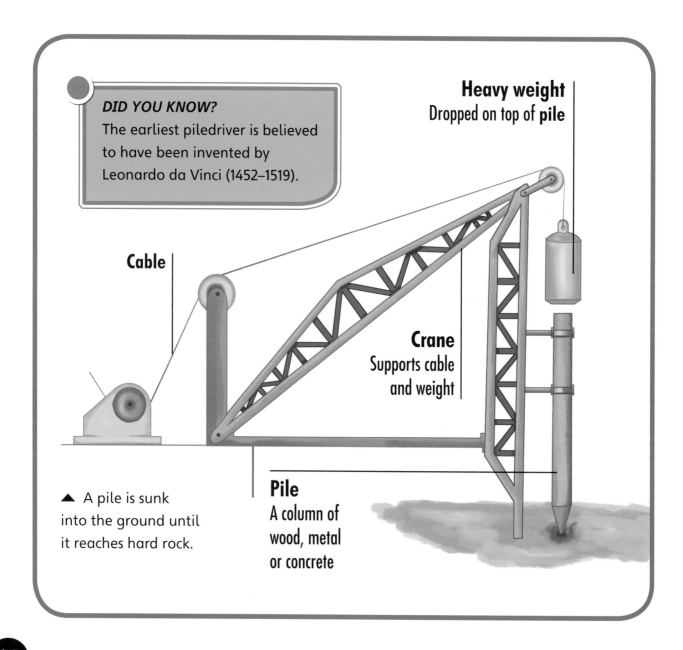

DID YOU KNOW?
The earliest piledriver is believed to have been invented by Leonardo da Vinci (1452–1519).

Heavy weight
Dropped on top of **pile**

Cable

Crane
Supports cable and weight

Pile
A column of wood, metal or concrete

▲ A pile is sunk into the ground until it reaches hard rock.

WHAT IS A PILE?

A pile is a heavy shaft of steel, concrete, or wood that is hammered into the ground to support a structure. Motorways, road and rail bridges, **highway overpasses**, and **embankments** are built on piles.

◀ Workers on a construction site get ready to sink a pile into the ground.

Pneumatic piledrivers use **compressed** air to raise a heavy piston inside a cylinder. The piston is dropped. The cylinder contains a mixture of fuel and air. **Friction** heats the mixture. The mixture ignites, forcing the piston back up. The cycle repeats until the machine is stopped.

Pipes
Force compressed air into cylinder

Crawler tracks
Keep vehicle from sinking into muddy ground

BLASTING

A **compressor** is like a pump, but instead of water, it pumps high-pressure air. Compressors can produce high-pressure air for sandblasters, which clean the outside of buildings. They can also power spray-painting machines, which produce an even coating of paint across a large wall or fence.

Sand blaster
Fires a high-pressure jet of water and sand at the wall

High above street level, a worker uses a pneumatic sandblaster to clean the side of a tall building.

DRILLING

Pneumatic drills used by construction crews work very much like compressed-air piledrivers. Instead of a hammer, the drills have tough steel blades to break up soil and tarmac. The air that works the pistons in a pneumatic drill is forced into the cylinder by a compressor.

◀ Air-driven machines are safer than electrical equipment because there is no danger of getting an electric shock, even in the rain.

HOW A PNEUMATIC DRILL WORKS

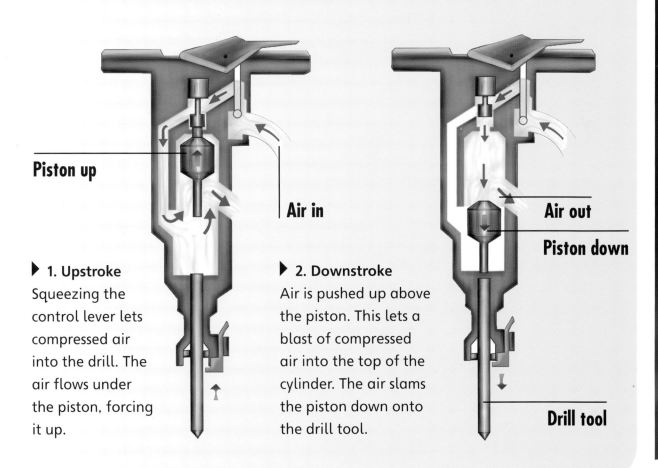

Piston up

Air in

Air out

Piston down

Drill tool

▶ **1. Upstroke**
Squeezing the control lever lets compressed air into the drill. The air flows under the piston, forcing it up.

▶ **2. Downstroke**
Air is pushed up above the piston. This lets a blast of compressed air into the top of the cylinder. The air slams the piston down onto the drill tool.

CRANES AND PULLEYS

Cranes use a series of simple pulleys to lift and move heavy weights, sometimes to the top of a building more than 20 stories high.

At any large construction site, you will see tall **cranes** towering above the skyline. At the base of the crane is a huge concrete block. Large bolts embedded deep in the concrete support the base and keep the crane firmly anchored to the ground.

▶ Construction crews use tower cranes to lift steel, concrete, bricks, building materials, and heavy tools such as generators from place to place.

Crane driver
Controls movement of **boom** and lifting gear

DID YOU KNOW?
The tallest tower cranes are more then 295 ft. (90 m) high. They are used to construct skyscrapers and other tall buildings.

HOW A PULLEY WORKS

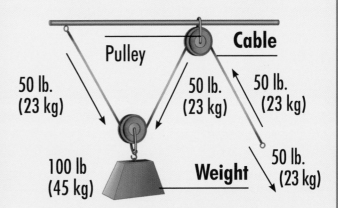

Pulley

Cable

50 lb. (23 kg)

50 lb. (23 kg)

50 lb. (23 kg)

100 lb (45 kg)

Weight

50 lb. (23 kg)

A double pulley system like this halves the effort needed to move a load, but the cable must be pulled twice as far.

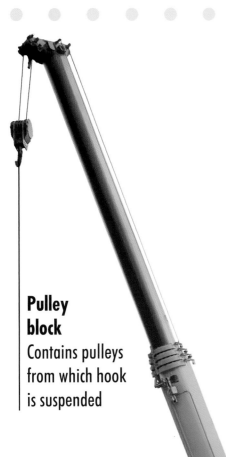

Pulley block
Contains pulleys from which hook is suspended

Boom or jib
Arm used to lift load

Hydraulic ram
Raises and lowers the boom or jib

Cab
For driving truck

◀ This mobile crane can move from place to place under its own power. The crane's hydraulic boom is like a telescope. It closes up when the crane is traveling.

Outrigger
Supports and steadies crane

Cab
For operating crane

HOW A CRANE BUILDS ITSELF

How is it that a crane is able to rise as the building grows taller? The answer is that a crane builds itself! First, the base is weighted with concrete and the **jib** is assembled on the ground. Then a mobile crane lifts a "climbing frame" onto the base. The cab and jib are put on top of the frame. The climbing frame has hydraulic rams, which raise the cab up to the height of each new section.

DID YOU KNOW?
The world's tallest free-standing tower crane stood 400 ft. (122 m) from the hook to the ground.

▼ A tower crane can build itself section by section. By adding new sections to itself, the crane can grow to match the height of the building being constructed.

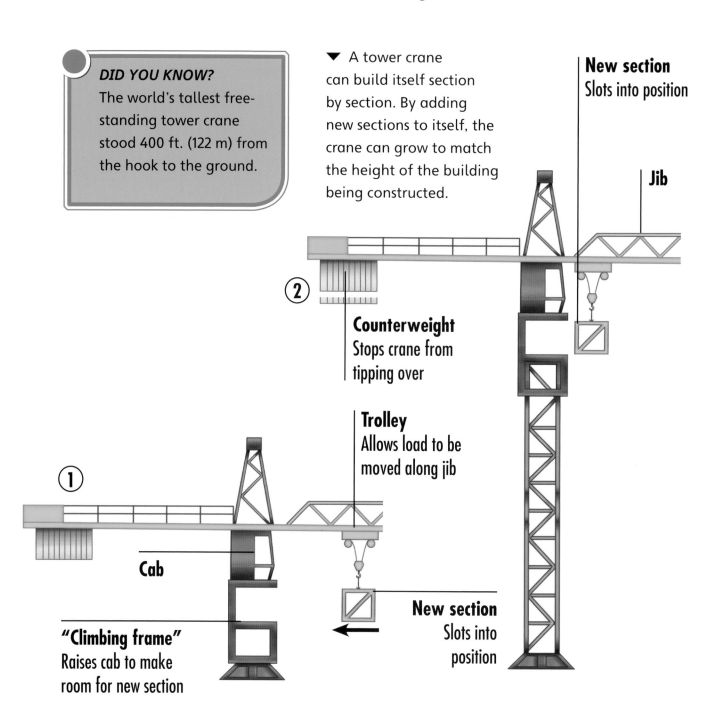

New section
Slots into position

Jib

Counterweight
Stops crane from tipping over

Trolley
Allows load to be moved along jib

Cab

"Climbing frame"
Raises cab to make room for new section

New section
Slots into position

DRIVING A CRANE

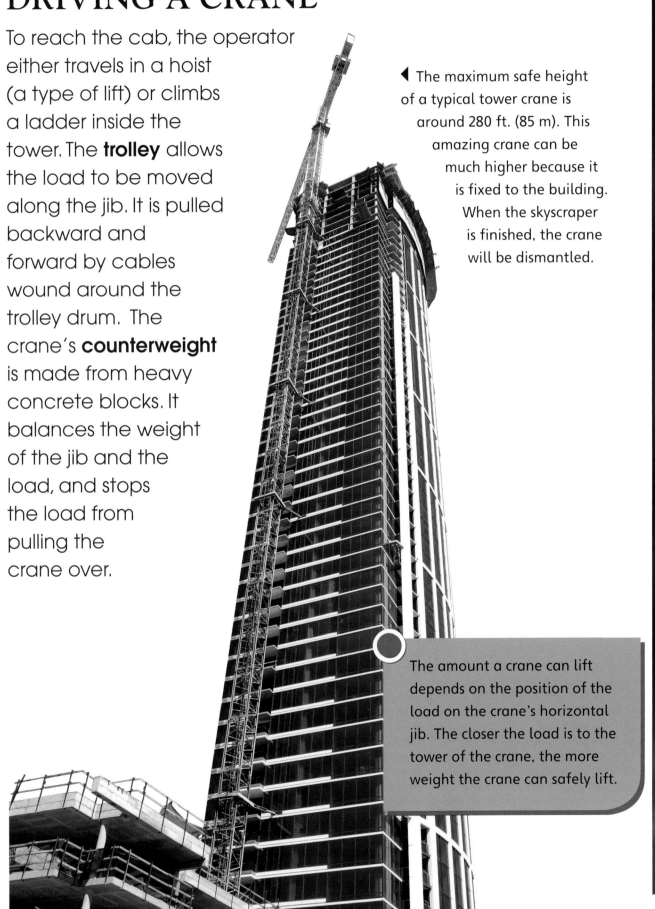

To reach the cab, the operator either travels in a hoist (a type of lift) or climbs a ladder inside the tower. The **trolley** allows the load to be moved along the jib. It is pulled backward and forward by cables wound around the trolley drum. The crane's **counterweight** is made from heavy concrete blocks. It balances the weight of the jib and the load, and stops the load from pulling the crane over.

◄ The maximum safe height of a typical tower crane is around 280 ft. (85 m). This amazing crane can be much higher because it is fixed to the building. When the skyscraper is finished, the crane will be dismantled.

The amount a crane can lift depends on the position of the load on the crane's horizontal jib. The closer the load is to the tower of the crane, the more weight the crane can safely lift.

SCREWS AND AUGERS

Did you know that screws not only hold things together, but they can also drill holes, carry a load, or pump up and mix materials?

AUGER DRILLS

Several construction machines use **screws** or **augers**. An auger is a screw with a wide **thread** that can be used to carry a load. A construction auger is used to drill holes for pipes or the piles for foundations. As the auger drills down, the soil spirals its way up along the thread. When the auger is full of soil, it is lifted out of the hole and cleared. It is then lowered back down to continue drilling.

▶ A construction auger is being used to drill a hole. Its thread has sharp edges to cut into the ground.

Rotary motor
Rotates auger as it cuts into ground

Auger
Cuts its way into ground like a corkscrew

MIXING CONCRETE

The drum of a concrete mixer truck contains a spiraling screw thread. When it turns one way, the spiraling screw thread inside mixes the concrete. When it turns the other way, the screw pushes the concrete to the mouth of the drum, ready for pouring.

Screw thread

Drum
Rotates about eight times a minute to mix concrete

▼ This mixer is pouring concrete onto a road.

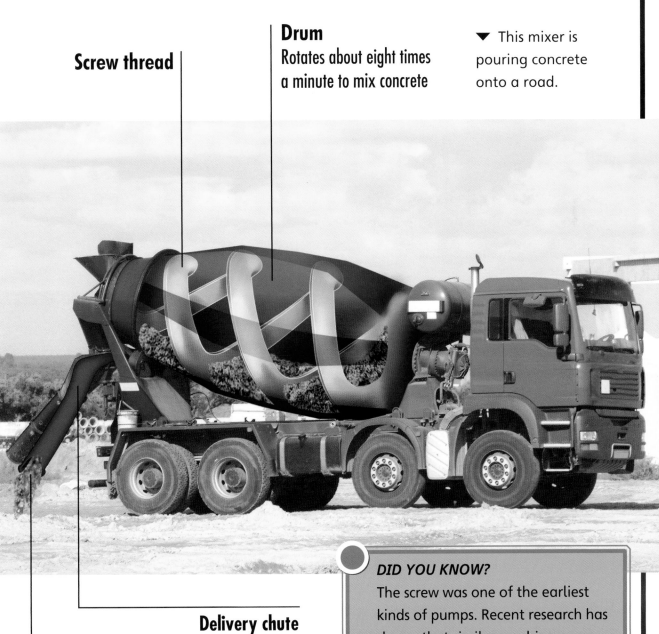

Concrete
Leveled by hand

Delivery chute
Weight of concrete makes it pour down metal chute from mouth of drum

DID YOU KNOW?
The screw was one of the earliest kinds of pumps. Recent research has shown that similar machines were used in the seventh century B.C.

GIANT DRILLS

Tunnel-boring machines (TBMs) are like giant drills. They can cut their way underground through soil, mud, and soft rocks. TBMs are used to build large tunnels to carry roads and railroad tracks through mountains, under cities, rivers, and even under the ocean. The TBM's cutting head is driven by a huge electric motor. As the head turns, its cutting rollers and teeth cut into the rock or soil ahead.

TUNNEL BORING MACHINE

Specification

Length:	39.4 ft. (2 m)
Weight:	882 tons (800 t)
Pressure on cutting head:	7,275 tons (6,600 t)
Max rate of removing waste rock and soil:	1,653 tons/hr (1,500 t/hr)

Control cab
Where the TBM operator sits

Moving belt
Carries the debris to railway trucks

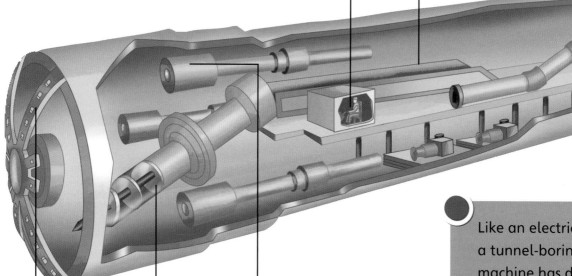

Like an electric drill, a tunnel-boring machine has different speeds to cut through different rocks.

Cutting head
Works like a drill driven by a huge electric motor

Auger
Rotates to carry away the cut soil and rock

Hydraulic rams
Force the cutting head forward into the rock or soil

WASTE

A long, rotating auger scoops up and carries the soil and ground-up rock from the TBM's cutting head. This waste is lifted onto a conveyor belt. The belt carries the waste back along the TBM and dumps it in railroad trucks. The railroad trucks take it out of the tunnel. As the TBM bores forward, huge concrete segments are fitted in place behind it to stop the tunnel from collapsing.

DID YOU KNOW?
The world's largest tunnel-boring machine began boring a tunnel under the Yangtze River in China in 2006. This TBM has a diameter of 50 ft. (15 m). The main cutting head alone weighs 187 tons (170 t).

Cutting head 11.5 ft. (3.5 m) in diameter to produce a finished tunnel 7.5 ft. (2.3 m) in diameter

Electric motors Rotate the cutting head

A tunnel-boring machine has created a new tunnel. All the TBM's systems are monitored by computers in the control cab. A laser system keeps the machine on course.

PUSHING AND SHOVING

Some of the toughest construction jobs are done by machines that push and shove. They use huge engines and steel blades to clear rocks, soil, and trees.

A bulldozer starts the work for a road, airport runway, or railway track. Its huge metal blade can clear anything in its path. The driver can angle the bulldozer's blade to control where soil and other materials are pushed. Bulldozers don't get stuck in mud because their weight is spread over wide **crawler tracks**.

Driver's cab
Strong steel frame protects driver if bulldozer rolls over

This large bulldozer is about to start clearing the site for a new road. The blade can be raised and lowered and tilted forward or backward, by a pair of hydraulic rams.

Blade
Made of solid steel

▼ Inside the cab of a bulldozer

Blade control joystick
Raises, lowers, and tilts the blade

Brake pedal
Adjusts the speed of the bulldozer and stops it

Steering wheel

DID YOU KNOW?
The engine exhaust of a bulldozer points upward to avoid damage from mud and rocks. Heavy steel prongs can be attached to the back of the bulldozer to break up hard ground.

SCRAPERS AND GRADERS

A grader has a cutting blade that is curved like a knife. Its job is to level the ground before a new road is laid. The grader's engine is nearly 10 times as powerful as a family car and twice as powerful as a bulldozer. The grader has huge, wide tires with deep treads to spread its weight and stop it from getting stuck on muddy ground. As it moves forward, the grader's knife-like blade slices off the top layer of soil and rubble.

▶ A grader is used to clear sites of rock and soil and to shape and level rough ground ready for building roads, buildings, and bridges.

Driver's cab

Hydraulic ram

Huge tires

Steel blade

GRADER

Specification

Length:	28.9 ft. (8.8 m)
Height:	10.5 ft. (3.2 m)
Engine:	165–185 **horsepower** diesel
Drive:	6 wheels (power drives all of the wheels, not just some of them)

HOLDING RUBBLE

In a scraper, soil and rubble are pushed into a container, called a bowl, by a conveyor belt of metal blades. The blades turn as the scraper moves. These metal blades, which move like the stairs of an escalator, are called the elevator. The scraper bowl can hold a load of more than 55 tons (50 t) of rubble.

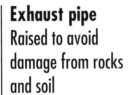

Exhaust pipe
Raised to avoid damage from rocks and soil

A grader levels the ground for a new road.

PAVING AND ROLLING

Road-paving machines are designed to lay a flat ribbon of asphalt road or airport runway. Any bumps would be a nightmare for fast traffic and aircraft.

Road-paving machines move very slowly. The **hopper** is a container that is constantly filled with steaming hot **asphalt**. Steel conveyor chains carry the asphalt to the rotating blades of the auger, which spread the asphalt on the ground.

VOGELE SUPER 2100-2 ROAD PAVER

Specification

Travel speed:	up to 2.8 mph (4.5 km/h)
Hopper size:	15.4 tons (14 t)
Max paving width:	42.6 ft. (13 m)
Paving speed:	82 ft. (25 m) per min

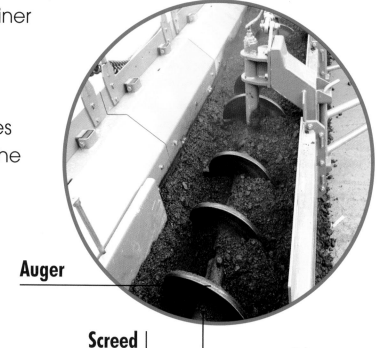

Auger

Screed
Flattens and smooths the asphalt

▶ A road paving machine.

▶ One set of road-paver controls drives the vehicle and another set controls laying the asphalt.

Controls
For conveyor, auger, and screed

Controls
For hopper and steering

IRONING THE ROAD

The road-paving machine also flattens and smooths the asphalt with a heavy vibrating attachment called the screed. This works a bit like a hot iron. Electric heaters inside the screed produce heat so that it creates a smooth finish to the asphalt.

Crawler tracks
Stop the paver from sinking in sticky asphalt

Hopper
Holds hot asphalt

A road-paving machine lays a new runway at Frankfurt Airport in Germany.

RAMMERS AND ROLLERS

To make a road strong and firm, it is made of many layers. Each layer must be flattened until it is hard and smooth. Rollers and rammers use weight and **vibrations** for this work. The greatest weight comes from a large roller. The roller is driven backward and forward over the layers of the road, flattening and smoothing them with its heavy wheels. The front and back wheels of rollers can be steered separately.

Roller drum
Rollers vibrate as the machine moves along

▼ This roller weighs about as much as eight family cars. Small water sprinklers above each roller keep them clean and cool.

Engine
Powerful 82 horsepower **diesel engine**

Water tank
Contains 96 gal. (365 L) of water to spray the rollers

CC222

TYPES OF ROLLERS

Smaller rollers are useful for laying pavements or repairing roads. The drum vibrates as it rolls, packing the surface below to make it really solid.

A rammer machine also vibrates to flatten strips of sand, gravel, or asphalt. It packs down the ground 10 times harder when it is vibrating than when it is still.

DID YOU KNOW?
The wheels of some rollers are hollow so that they can be filled with water or sand to increase the weight.

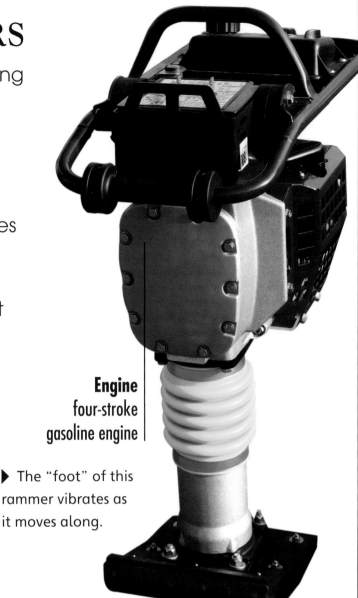

Engine
four-stroke gasoline engine

▶ The "foot" of this rammer vibrates as it moves along.

Controls

Twin drum vibrating roller

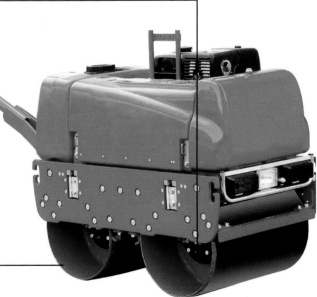

▶ This small vibrating roller is useful for laying pavements and repairing roads.

Twin drum vibrating roller

GLOSSARY

Asphalt A sticky, tarry substance that is mixed with gravel or crushed rock to surface roads, airport runways, and playgrounds

Auger A tool, like a large corkscrew, for boring holes in the ground or for carrying loose materials

Boom The long, extending arm of a crane

Bucket The scoop of an excavator

Compressed Squeezed or pressed together

Compressor A machine that squashes or squeezes air into a smaller space

Counterweight A metal or concrete weight attached to a crane, which balances the load to stop the crane from falling over

Crane A machine that is used to lift heavy objects

Crawler track A wide metal belt around a set of wheels that helps a machine to move over soft or slippery ground

Cylinder Part of an engine in which a piston moves

Diesel engine An engine that works by burning oil

Embankment A supporting ridge often made of soil or stone

Excavator A machine that digs holes

Friction A force produced when two surfaces rub together

Highway overpass A section of a road that crosses over another route

Hopper A container for carrying loads

Horsepower (hp) A unit for measuring the power of an engine

Hydraulic A system for operating machines that uses a liquid to push pistons and make the machine work

Jack A device for lifting something heavy off the ground